TO THE GRADY COUNTY
SHERIFF'S DEPARTMENT

MAY THE GOOD LORD BE YOUR
GUIDING LIGHT IN ALL THAT YOU
DO. AND PROTECT YOU AS YOU
PERFORM YOUR DUTIES FOR THE
CITIZENS OF GRADY COUNTY!

CRAIG'S STORY

STEWART AND BETH ANN MEYER

WESTBOW
PRESS®
A DIVISION OF THOMAS NELSON
& ZONDERVAN

WestBow Press books may be ordered through booksellers or by contacting:

WestBow Press
A Division of Thomas Nelson & Zondervan
1663 Liberty Drive
Bloomington, IN 47403
www.westbowpress.com
1 (866) 928-1240

ISBN: 978-1-5127-7618-8 (sc)
ISBN: 978-1-5127-7620-1 (hc)
ISBN: 978-1-5127-7619-5 (e)

Library of Congress Control Number: 2017902639

Print information available on the last page.

WestBow Press rev. date: 2/27/2017

To Izzie Butler (Craig's daughter),

Deserae "Des" Butler (our daughter-in-law),

and Christy Schroeder (our daughter)

Acknowledgments

We wrote *Craig's Story*, a true story about our son, to help those who are grieving for a loved one and to help people understand those who are going through the grieving process.

When you first lose someone you love, the hurt is so hard that it feels physical. The hurt will remain, but the pain softens as time passes. Life becomes more bearable. Losing a loved one is something you never get over. We hope this book will make each day easier to bear.

We want to thank our family and friends for their support:

- Our daughter Christy, Brandon Schroeder, and their children Zak, Alex, and Abby

- Our daughter-in-law Deserae, Zack Butler, and their children Izzie, Tinleigh, and Owen

- Des's parents, Perry and Kathy Wenzel

- Tammi Bailey, Kendall and Paula Brashears, Tom and Janice Boyt, Bob and Sheila Suvino, Scott and Rhonda Tack, Steven and Kay Winn, and Brandon and Melinda Barton

- The late retired Oklahoma City Assistant Fire Chief Jon Hansen

- The biggest family of all—the Oklahoma Highway Patrol

- The Arkansas State Police and Trooper David Jones

- Batesville Regional Airport

- The community of Chickasha, Oklahoma

- First Baptist Church of Chickasha

- Chickasha Public Schools

- Barr Air Patrol

Craig Stewart Meyer

May 12, 1980–January 4, 2007

On Thursday afternoon, January 4, 2007, we received a call from our daughter-in-law, Deserae, telling us that Craig's plane was missing. Craig and his flying partner had left Indiana that morning. They were to have landed at Batesville, Arkansas to fuel up. They never made it.

Craig and Deserae were living in McKinney, Texas, so Stewart and I packed up and headed there. Des's parents (Perry and Kathy) were on their way too. Through phone conversations in the car, Stewart and Perry decided to head to Arkansas. Perry came back from Des's house and met us in Sherman, Texas, which was about thirty minutes from McKinney. Stewart got in with Perry, and I went to Des's house. Izzie was seven months old, and she thought it was wonderful having "Mimi" (Kathy) and "BamMa" (me) there to play with her.

We were so thankful for the weather. The temperature had been in the sixties and would continue that way. One comfort came from the full moon. We could look at the moon and know that the same moon was also looking over Craig.

Stewart and Perry drove to Edmond, Oklahoma, and spent the night with Jon Hansen. On Friday morning, they went to Wiley Post Airport. As soon as the fog cleared, the highway patrol pilot flew them to Batesville.

Des and I were pacing, wanting to be in Arkansas. Kathy said she'd stay with Izzie. Des and I left for Batesville on Friday morning. We took Highway 75 to eastern Oklahoma.

We saw so many signs of Craig along the way. He loved American flags, and we saw them in so many unusual places … up on the hill, made out of rocks, and in the field. We passed "Craig Trailers." We could feel Craig with us.

We kept in constant contact with our daughter. Christy

had also been following the progress on the TV and the Internet.

Stewart, Jon, Perry, Major Larry Alexander (OHP), and the pilots, Trooper Jerry Green and Trooper John Girten, had landed at Batesville. That is when Stewart got the news that they had found the plane. There were no survivors.

Des and I were about thirty minutes away from Jay, Oklahoma when Stewart called and told us the news. Des and I parked on the side of the road, feeling the impact of the message. In Jay, a highway patrolman picked us up and took us to the Grove airport. Craig's flight company was waiting for us with a plane to take us to Batesville. The plane was just like the one Craig had been flying. It was very hard for us to get in the plane, but we managed. As I was holding Des's left hand, I looked down at her ring. It hit me that Des was a widow.

It had been foggy and cloudy all day, but after about thirty minutes of being in the air, the sky cleared up. The sun started shining. We smiled and felt Craig with us. We also felt God's comfort. When we landed, we said, "That was for Craig." We knew he'd be proud of us.

Stewart, Jon, Perry, Larry, the pilots, and David Jones (an Arkansas state trooper) were at the airport. Our niece Melinda had driven up with her husband Brandon Barton. Brandon was prepared to hike through the hills in search of the plane. The airport lounge was filled with submarine sandwiches, KFC, pop, and water.

Motel arrangements had been made for us all at the Comfort Inn Suites in Batesville. Our friends, Bob and Sheila Suvino, drove from Fayetteville, Arkansas, and spent the night too.

On Friday morning, they had discovered the plane about one mile south of the Batesville airport. The plane had hit the treetops, flipped over, and landed upside down. Weather may have played a factor.

Jon went to the crash site with the team. When he got to the plane, he cut off Craig's seat belt and pulled him gently out of the plane. Jon held him and talked to him. That was such a comfort to us. Jon said he only had a few cuts and scratches. The impact had killed them instantly.

On Saturday, we all went to the crash site. They had made a mile-long trail to get to the plane. We walked all around the plane and saw Craig's lunch box, coat, water bottle, and phone cord. We walked toward the slope and saw a white church steeple in the distance.

We could feel Craig telling us everything was okay. Des and I noticed the pretty rocks. We both picked up rocks to take with us. We got one for Christy and the kids. As we left the site, we continued to feel the peace of God's comfort and Craig's presence. Before we left, we all got in a circle, held hands, and prayed.

We received a lot of calls on our cell phones, and we kept checking our answering machine at home. Most everyone said, "We are praying for you." We felt such comfort and truly felt the prayers. It was the best message anyone could receive at a time like that.

Trooper David Jones was off on Saturday, but he spent

the day with us and took us where we needed to go. We went to the Criminal Investigation Division of the Independence County Sheriffs' office, and they released Craig's belongings to Des. His lunch box contained two apples, a fruit cup, pretzels, and a yogurt (our inspiration for healthy eating). They also gave her his coat, planner book (with Izzie's picture on the front), watch, wallet, ChapStick, and dental floss.

We were touched when he handed her Craig's wedding ring—the one she had given him on their wedding day. It was a symbol of their union. She quietly slipped it onto her own finger. With this ring, till death do us part. They had looked through his suitcase. They said, "His clothes are okay—and so are his PlayStation and games." We had to laugh at that. Des said anytime he went on an overnight flight, he brought his PS2 because he never had time to play it at home.

On Saturday afternoon, it was time to go home. However, none of us had cars. Perry's car was at Jon Hansen's house. Des and I had driven in her mother's car on Friday, but a trooper had picked it up at the airport and taken it back to Chickasha.

We thought of flying back to McKinney but decided against it. An OHP plane took Perry back to Edmond so he could get his car. Bob and Sheila drove us to Cercy, Arkansas, and Jon rented a minivan for us. Jon drove Stewart, Des, and me back to McKinney.

At first, we were thinking about how long the drive would be (seven hours), but God knew we needed that time. We planned the entire service arrangements. We were able to call the ministers and make arrangements for the music. Christy was able to help us with ideas over the phone. All the planning was written on McDonald's napkins. We were constantly calling Kendall and Paula Brashears for information about how to get in touch with preachers and other things. Des kept in close contact with her mother, Kathy, and Izzie. Kathy took care of phone calls and the media there.

We arrived in McKinney at eleven on Saturday night. We gave Des time with Izzie, and then Stewart and I had our turn. She had been asleep and was so cuddly. It felt so good to hold her. We sometimes called Isabella "Craigabella" because she looked so much like her daddy.

Perry had driven from Edmond to McKinney. Everyone helped us load up Craig's model airplanes, his rocking airplane (Uncle Mike made for him when he was two), pictures, and everything else we wanted for the service. At one in the morning, Jon, Stewart, and I returned the rental car, got in our loaded-down Excursion, and headed home.

When we arrived home at five on Sunday morning, the cross on our hill was shining brightly. When Craig was sixteen, he had built it and lit it every Christmas and Easter. Our lights had burned out, but our neighbor, Scott Tack, had wrapped it with new lights.

After we slept for about an hour and a half, Stewart and I decided to go to church. The service was just what we needed—and so were the hugs. Christy, Brandon, and their kids gave us the biggest hugs that afternoon. Abby, Alex, and Zak had just seen Craig on December 27. Stewart and I had taken the kids to Texas to spend a few days with Craig and

Des. Craig and Des took the kids to Six Flags on Wednesday, and we stayed home with Izzie. They took them on every roller coaster (Abby's favorite), and when they got back to the house, Alex said, "This was the best day of my life."

We were going to leave Texas on Thursday (December 28), but Craig and Des had asked us to stay until Friday. On Friday morning, Craig had an early flight. He came into our bedroom, hugged and kissed us, and told us he loved us. What a wonderful memory.

Craig's service was on Wednesday, January 10, 2007. As we were planning the service on the way home, Des asked for Craig's former youth minister, Brad Davis, to do the service. Stan Warfield read the scripture. He was Craig and Des's minister at United Methodist in Stillwater, Oklahoma. Our preacher, Johnny Tims, gave the eulogy. We had a slideshow of Craig's life. Stewart shared many of our family memories, as I stood by his side.

Des requested a closed casket. We wanted everyone to

remember Craig's smile. We had a lot of poster-sized pictures of Craig and Craig with his family.

Craig was buried in Rush Springs, Oklahoma. Des had lost her great-grandfather the previous summer. When they went to the gravesite after Gramp's funeral, Craig and Des commented that they would like to be buried there. The cemetery overlooked miles of hills and trees.

Des and Izzie moved back to Chickasha on Sunday, January 7, 2007. When she found out Craig didn't make it, she said, "I'm moving back to Chickasha." Her family packed up all their furniture and belongings.

Des and Izzie were surrounded by family and friends. We are so lucky to have them close to us now. And Craig will *always* be with us.

Craig's sister, Christy, and her family live in El Reno, Oklahoma. She and Craig were so close. Their only fight was Bedlam. Craig was a huge Oklahoma State University fan, and Christy is a huge Oklahoma University fan. The OSU Pokes won their bowl game, and the OU Sooners lost their bowl game on January 1. Craig e-mailed Christy on January 2:

> How about them Sooners?! Go Pokes!
> Love, your baby brother

We're so thankful we had twenty-six wonderful years with Craig. We have no doubt that he is in heaven—and we know how happy he is. His belief in God was so strong. His smile will never stop.

Power of Prayer

We've always believed in the power of prayer, but it was never stronger than when we were searching for Craig. As soon as Des called to tell us that Craig's plane was missing, we began praying. We immediately called Christy and the rest of our family. We called and sent messages to the rest of our family and friends. The subject line was "Pray for Craig."

I can't begin to guess the number of people who were praying. For twenty-four hours, we prayed, "Please, Lord, just let us find Craig alive." When we found Craig and realized he hadn't made it, we were devastated. The power of prayer brought us through the pain. It was as if God took all the prayers that went up for Craig, wove them into a quilt, and wrapped us in it. The comfort we drew from that "quilt" was unbelievable.

It gave us a whole new perspective to the power of prayer.

Just because everyone is praying for a specific answer doesn't mean that God is going to give us that answer. It means that he will give us the strength to handle whatever his answer is.

The Crash Site

With Craig's strong feeling of patriotism, we found it ironic that the crash site was in Independence County, Arkansas.

The next morning, we were having breakfast and talking about the crash site. Craig and the other pilot had already been moved to town. It had taken a while to find the plane because of its location in the hills and canyon. Once they located the plane by air, they had to clear a "road" to the site. We all got in cars and drove toward the site, finishing in all-terrain vehicles.

It was very hard to walk up to Craig's plane and see where he and the other pilot had been. There was a lot of debris in the trees and all around the plane. All of a sudden, we noticed the peacefulness in the area. The church in the hills was God's way of telling us that he was taking care of Craig for us.

We found a water bottle on the ground and wanted any part of Craig we could find. We felt at peace when we left Craig's plane. As we prayed in a circle, we felt Craig and God's presence.

Our First Sunday Back in Church

We added on to our house in 1983. A good friend, Garland, was our builder. Stewart and I were his helpers. Garland loved to sing while he worked. One of his favorite songs was "Sweet, Sweet Spirit." He would be singing, and it wasn't long before Stewart was singing with him. It became one of our favorite songs. Stewart even sang it in church. On the Sunday after Craig died, we went to church. The first song the congregation sang was "Sweet, Sweet Spirit." We weren't able to sing, but we absorbed every word. The song held such a special meaning, especially since Garland had passed away several years earlier. What a message from God! "We are all good here."

A Celebration of Life

Craig's service was on January 10, 2007. The church was full of family and friends. A few days before the service, we went to Des's family's cobblestone house in the country. We needed quiet time for our family to reflect on Craig. With Christy, Des, and her family, we came up with wonderful memories to share at his service. Craig's service was a celebration of life. Stewart and I were able to share the family stories at the service.

Mr. Mustard

There were so many beautiful flowers, plants, and mementoes at Craig's service, but one stood out in particular. When Craig was young, Stewart and Jon Hansen took him to an 89ers baseball game in Oklahoma City. As they were walking to their seats, Craig saw a mustard packet on the ground. He stomped on it, and mustard shot all over Stewart and Jon. He looked at them and grinned.

From then on, Jon called him "Mr. Mustard." It became his nickname, and Craig used it in his e-mail address. At the service, there was a beautiful wreath. From a distance, there appeared to be yellow flowers all over the wreath. However, on closer inspection, it was actually mustard packets—from Jon.

Craig's Rocking Plane

Craig was destined to be a pilot. From the time he was little, his favorite toys were planes. When he was two and a half, his uncle made him a rocking airplane. Mike and Lynette gave it to Craig for Christmas. He sat in it and very seriously said, "It won't fly."

When he graduated from high school, he jokingly asked for a 152 Cessna. At least we think it was a joke because he didn't get one.

Nanny

Heaven is getting sweeter all the time. Stewart's mother, Joyce, had been sick for several years. In May 2007, she knew she didn't have much time left. Before she passed away, she said, "The first thing I'll do when I get to heaven is hug and kiss Craig for you."

Handling the "After"

Stewart and I bought a Bible after we were married. We recorded our wedding and the birth of our children. In the front of our Bible, we recorded the death of Stewart's sister. Every Sunday in church, I would look at our Bible and think, *I need to put Craig's name in there with Marilynn's.* But I just couldn't make myself do it. One Sunday I told Stewart, "This is the day I'm going to write his name in the Bible." I opened up first to the births to see Craig and Christy's names. When I turned the page to write his name, I just stared at it. It was already written down—in my own handwriting. I have no idea when I did that.

Everything was such a blur after his death. We couldn't remember simple things such as when to take the trash down to the road. We decided to keep a notebook on the kitchen counter and write down everything we needed to do. It was a good thing we had an automatic dog feeder or we might have had to write that down too.

Make a list. Don't take it for granted that you will

remember. Write it down and cross it off when it's complete.

The first time I crossed something off my list, I thought, *I accomplished something.* Something so simple made me feel better.

Take some time off. Craig's accident was on a Thursday, and his service was the following Wednesday. I was planning to go back to work the following Monday. However, the weather had different plans. A major ice and snowstorm hit on Friday, shutting down many things in Oklahoma, including the schools. I was home for an additional week. We used the time to write thank-you notes. Writing the notes was a time-consuming activity, but it was also very therapeutic. I had written a journal about Craig (the journal is at the beginning of this book). To those who sent something but did not attend the service, I sent a copy of the journal and a copy of the service program.

Dealing with Reality

We will never get over losing Craig. After all these years, it still hurts. But it doesn't hurt as hard. It's a day-to-day process.

We ask God daily to get us through the day. At night, we thank him because he did.

January 4, 2007, sometimes seems like yesterday. We look at each other and say, "Can you believe he's gone?" At other times, it seems like forever ago. Would we bring him back today if we could? The selfish and human part of us says, "Absolutely!" But since that is not a possibility, we don't dwell on it. As believers in Christ, we know Craig is in heaven. We are at complete peace and know we will see him again.

We are so blessed to have Izzie. When Des was pregnant, I wanted the baby to have her green eyes. Everyone in our family has brown eyes, and Izzie has her daddy's brown eyes. We see so much of Craig in Izzie. You just can't beat that.

I Don't Get It

Years ago, I tutored a student after school. We were working on a lesson about adding and subtracting fractions. He was doing every problem correctly, but he kept saying, "I don't get it." I kept saying, "But you are getting them right." He finally looked me in the eye and said, "Mrs. Meyer, I know *how* to work the problems but I don't know *why*. I don't get it." We put the worksheet aside and found some paper plates. We sat on the floor and cut the paper plates into pieces of pie, adding and subtracting the pieces. Soon, he said, "I get it now."

So many times, Stewart and I said, "I don't get it." We knew Craig was gone, but we didn't get it. Wouldn't it be wonderful if God could sit down on the floor with us and explain everything?

Counseling

Stewart had just retired from the Oklahoma Highway Patrol when we lost Craig. I was still teaching. I would go to school, and Stewart would be home. It was very difficult. He had too much quiet time on his hands. At times, he would come to school and get me for lunch. It would be very hard for him to go back home. It was a very difficult semester.

We thought we were strong enough to get through it ourselves, but we weren't. Sometimes God gives you an extra push and says, "Hey, you all have to do something." In the highway patrol, you are part of a huge family. The highway patrol has a full-time psychologist. We called and made an appointment. Craig had died at noon. That day, we had gone to the store, watched TV, and worked on the computer—not knowing we had lost Craig. I said, "As a mother, shouldn't I have felt something?" I felt so guilty that I had spent five hours living normally. And Craig was gone. The psychologist said, "How could you?"

Stewart was concerned about how scared Craig would have been in those last few moments.

She said, "Just like your training with the highway patrol, his training kicked in—and that's what he would have been concentrating on."

Counseling is not a sign of weakness. It's another way of letting God do his job. We considered it a gift.

Many local towns have counseling available. "Grief Share" is available in many churches. It has been helpful to us. We have been able to share *Craig's Story* in different churches, which is helpful to us and hopefully helpful to others.

Cards and Gifts

I never realized the importance of receiving cards. In the first few weeks, we received many cards. We opened them together when we could. I cut the addresses off the envelopes and taped them to each card. We handled the cards off and on for months. I even put them in alphabetical order by sender because it gave me another excuse to touch them. We keep them in a special bag with Craig's things. They are never forgotten. Just glancing at the bag when I walk by gives me comfort. Maybe I will put them in a scrapbook someday.

I remember the first day we did not receive a card in the mail, and it made me feel sad. The reality hit me. Life goes on as usual. However, months later, we received another card. The timing could have not been better. We still get one every now and then from someone who is thinking of us.

One thing we learned from receiving cards is that they

are an invisible hug. It's a small effort for someone to make, but it means so much. It does not matter how late you send a card. Knowing that someone is thinking about you gives you strength. It's that "quilt" that is wrapped around you.

We received cards, flowers, and food. It was wonderful not having to worry about feeding family and friends. Most of all, it was a comfort to know that people cared. It is very important to write thank-you notes. I would like to stress the importance of putting your name and address on whatever you send. I had to search for a number of addresses, but it meant so much to us to be able to say thank you.

Letting Others Help

Allow people to help you in any way they can—whether it's making phone calls or running errands.

A day or two after we were back, many of my teacher friends came over to help with food and drinks. We had a lot of visitors, and the teachers were ready for the first request.

My dad asked me for a drink of water, and five teachers went to the kitchen to get it for him.

A lady from church came over and said, "Give me your laundry." Like an obedient child, I went for it. She brought all the clean laundry back the next day—folded and ready to be put away.

A teacher friend said, "If you leave for a few hours, I'll come clean your house." It didn't take long for us to find a place to go. Coming home to a clean house was wonderful.

Another friend asked if she could make a scrapbook of Craig. She said she had done it for other family members who had lost children. She spent hours with the pictures we gave her and made a wonderful keepsake.

A couple called and said, "We want to take you out to eat. We have a place in mind—we just need you to tell us the day." We had a great dinner and a great visit.

We didn't know what we needed. We were in a daze. If you want to help someone, think of something that would help you. If you say, "Let me know what I can do for you," they usually will not come up with anything. We appreciate everything that was done for us.

Many of our family and friends have gone through illness, tragedies, or the death of a family member or friend. I can't tell you the number of times we have said, "Let me know what we can do to help."

People may not ask because they are afraid or embarrassed. They might not know what they need. They might be in the position to be "givers" and not "takers." They might be afraid of being turned down.

After Craig died, friends brought food, paper goods, bottled water, and postage stamps. For weeks, the kindness never ended. If someone had asked how to help us, I never would have suggested doing my laundry, cleaning our house, or taking us out to eat.

When people are grieving, they might have no idea what they need. A suggestion might open their eyes and make them say, "Oh, yes, that sounds great." If someone offers a suggestion or gift, it is up to you to decide if you want to accept it.

A friend had surgery recently, and I sent a text to see how he was doing. After he answered, I asked if there was anything we could do. He said he was fine. A few minutes later, I sent another text: "We are headed to Sonic. Can we bring you anything?"

He said, "Yes! A large Dr. Pepper."

If you truly want to do something for someone, think about what you would like and what you are willing to do.

I Don't Know What To Say

We went to the store a week after Craig's service. We ran into many people we knew, and we got many hugs. Then something strange happened. A lady I knew walked down a different aisle after she saw us. I knew she had seen us. Then it dawned on me. She didn't know what to say to us. It didn't upset me, but it did make me realize that some people just don't know how to respond in that situation.

We never got tired of people saying, "I'm so sorry," "I'm thinking of you," or "I'm praying for you." A hug requires no words. Some people couldn't express their thoughts in words, but they conveyed their messages with hugs.

It's never too late to offer condolences. I ran into one of Christy's classmates years later. She came up to me and told me how sorry she was about Craig. That meant so much for two reasons. First, it showed me that she cared. Second, it told me that Craig was not forgotten.

We may feel like it's our duty to make someone feel better. It's easy to tell people all the reasons their loved one was taken, how they are in a better place, or how they are not suffering anymore. In reality it sounds good—and it is correct—but when the hurt is still an open wound, just give that person a hug.

We love it when someone mentions Craig, but not everyone wants that "reminder."

Do you want to ask someone about a loved one, but you aren't sure if the person wants to talk about it? Here is a simple conversation starter: "I've been thinking about you. How are you doing?" (They know what you are referring to.) They might reply one of two ways:

1. "I'm fine." If they start talking about something else, you know that topic is closed.
2. "Thanks for asking." If they start talking about their loved ones, the topic is open.

Take the cue from them. It's okay if they start crying when you ask. Sometimes we need a good cry with a good friend— and people cry whether someone reminds them or not.

Awkward Situations

We had so many thank-you letters to write. We went to the store and bought twenty packages of thank-you notes. The lady checking us out made several comments: "Wow. You have a lot of thank you notes to write. You must have had a really big party." With each comment, I just smiled. "Was it a birthday party?" I had to answer. I said, "No, we just lost our son and have a lot of thank you notes to write." She didn't know what to say.

Our daughter-in-law had a similar experience when she went shopping for a black dress. When she went to check out, the clerk said, "What a pretty dress. That's going to look cute on you. Are you going to a party?" Des said, "No, I'm going to my husband's funeral."

None of the incidents were meant to be hurtful, but they made everyone involved feel badly. We all need to be careful. If you don't get much of a response from one comment, it probably needs to end there, especially for people who work in some kind of service capacity.

Craig's Birthday and "Angelversary"

Christy and Craig were always so close. Their biggest argument was about football. As the first anniversary of his death was approaching, Christy said, "We need to think of a way to celebrate each year. How about if we call January 4 his *angelversary*?" It make us smile when we say that.

Since then, we use angelversary for Stewart's parents, sister, and other loved ones.

If you think about them on their birthday or angelversary, it's okay to say something. Someone once said, "I didn't want to say anything to remind you and make you sad." It's this simple: we never forget. It's a good feeling for someone else to remember. And if it makes us cry, that's okay too. That's just part of the healing process.

Visiting the Cemetery

We don't have a set time to visit the cemetery. Craig's birthday is May 12. That is usually the time we are either "Walking to Stillwater" or working the Summer Games for Special Olympics. Just because we can't make it to the cemetery doesn't mean we can't still remember him wherever we are. The same thing applies to his angelversary. We make it to the cemetery when we can. We don't choose to add pressure by feeling like we have to make a visit on a certain day.

The Cotton Bowl (Stewart)

We arrived in Arlington, Texas, the evening before the Cotton Bowl and were ready for a late dinner. When we entered the restaurant in our OSU shirts, another family was waiting to be seated. They happened to be wearing Mississippi shirts.

The hostess could have seated us anywhere in that large restaurant, but she chose to seat us next to our opponent. It didn't take long to strike up a conversation with the parents and their daughter. We told them that our son had graduated from OSU, and the father asked what he did now. We told them we had lost him in a plane accident. They expressed their sorrow and began speaking about their son who had committed suicide. It's hard to know what to say when you lose a son or daughter, but under those circumstances, it was extremely difficult. Not really knowing what to say, we offered our condolences by just saying we were sorry. I remember touching his shoulder, and he was rigid. It wasn't long before he started crying. He had not been able to do before, and it was much needed.

At times like those, you realize that God gave us the appropriate words and actions to say and use. He had a table reserved just for us.

The Alamo Bowl

We arrived in San Antonio early so we could participate in the activities before the Oklahoma State University and University of Texas at San Antonio game. We attended a banquet with all the captains, teams, spirit squads, mascots, and bands. There was no reserved seating, but we noticed a table with room for the two of us. We sat down next to a couple and introduced ourselves. It's amazing how many times people ask, "Do you have children?" They told us their son was on the OSU team. They had lost their daughter to complications from surgery.

We told them we had a daughter but had lost our son. We spent most of dinner talking about our children. We discovered that we had lost our children within a week of each other. We wear a bracelet with Craig's name. They were wearing a bracelet with their daughter's name. We have continued a relationship with them throughout the years.

Death Notification (Stewart)

One of the most difficult responsibilities we had as troopers was contacting a family to make a death notification. We were taught to be sensitive to the needs of the individuals we contacted. If people came up to us at accident scenes after their loved ones had already been transported, we would advise them that the loved ones were being taken care of. We would try to wait until we were at the emergency room with health care professionals in case care was needed for the loved ones.

People react in different ways when they lose loved ones. They faint, go into shock, cry, or scream. I even had a mother start beating on my chest and yelling, "You said my daughter was being taken care of!" I will never forget that one. I often wondered how I would react on the receiving end of a death notification.

I flew to Batesville with Jon, Perry, Major Larry Alexander, John Girten, and Jerry Green to search for Craig's plane. We landed somewhere between Oklahoma City and Batesville. Major Larry Alexander got off the plane and was talking to two men who appeared to be officers. I was glad Larry was with us. He had lost a brother who was a state trooper in the line of duty in a plane crash on July 3, 1978. I was a young trooper and had been in the field since May. It really had a sobering affect on me. Five troopers had lost their lives in the line of duty between January and May 1978.

When we landed in Batesville, everyone exited the plane except for Larry and me. Larry came back to where I was seated, put a hand on my shoulder, and told me there were no survivors. He told me how sorry he was. I told him I needed to be by myself for a few minutes. I remember thinking that I needed to be in control of myself when I get off the plane. I lowered my head and cried. It is so difficult to be on the receiving end.

I knew there was so much to do, and I needed to prepare myself for what was to come. I had to notify Beth Ann, Des, Christy, and the rest of the family. I prayed for strength and the right words to say.

My instincts told me I needed to tell them in person, but I couldn't figure out a way to do it. I knew that Beth Ann and Des had started driving to Batesville. I contacted Beth Ann by phone. I told them that Craig had not survived the crash. I told her a trooper would meet them and take them to the nearest airport. The company Craig worked for would pick them up and bring them to Batesville. I called Christy and told her. I wish I could have been there to wrap my arms around Beth Ann, Christy, and Des. I felt useless.

It is not easy to be on the receiving end of a death notification. I was fortunate that the good Lord put Larry, Jon, and Perry in my life that day. Having friends and family in your life during a loss is so important—and so is being there for someone who needs you.

Photography credit Michelle Wiginton

Scrapbook credit Tammi Bailey

Notifying Loved Ones

It's difficult to let loved ones know about a death. What made it even more difficult for us was that we had to let almost everyone know by phone.

Stewart called Des, Christy, and me. Des and I had to wait until we landed in Batesville to make more calls.

Stewart called his dad. His mother was in a nursing home at the time. He did not want to call his mother. Instead, the highway patrol went to Stewart's dad's house. They took him to the nursing home so he could tell Joyce in person.

I didn't want my parents to hear about Craig over the phone. I called my brother, and Belford went to their house to tell them.

When I called our preacher, Johnny Tims, he said, "Baby, I'm so sorry." That's what I needed. I'll never forget what his words did for me.

No matter how you notify someone, it's never easy. Several people offered to make calls for us. That helped. It was nice to have others call extended family and friends.

When someone has mentioned losing a loved one, I often think, *Thank God for memories.* Here are a few of those memories:

Merry Christmas (1980)

For Craig's first Christmas, he was seven months old. Christy was four. She woke us up at four o'clock in the morning to tell us that Santa had visited.

We watched Christy open her gifts and helped Craig open his. Christy got the newly popular Strawberry Shortcake dolls, including a dollhouse. Craig received the usual baby toys.

Stewart's family came over for Christmas. We had lunch and opened our gifts from the family. Stewart's sister Marilynn and her baby (Melinda) left after that. She let Michelle stay so she and Christy could play more.

Stewart was on call and had to report for duty at three o'clock. Christy, Craig, Michelle, and I rode home to Clinton with his parents. Stewart's dad was driving, and Nanny was holding Craig in the front seat. (There were no child restraint or seat belt laws then.) We turned north on Highway 81 from Chickasha, and Nanny handed Craig to me.

When we came close to the intersection by Airport Road, a car ran the stop sign. With no way to avoid it, we hit him broadside. Joyce and Bill were both thrown into the windshield. Craig, Christy, Michelle, and I were thrown against the backs of the front seat. No one was wearing seat belts. (Of course, we are never without them now.) Several people stopped to help us. Stewart's parents were conscious but incoherent. The children and I seemed fine, but we were sore and shaken up.

Someone notified the highway patrol. I thought, *Stewart is on call and will be on his way.* I hated the thought of him arriving on the scene and finding out his family was involved. I walked to the nearest farmhouse and asked if I could use their phone. Thank goodness he answered. He let me know he could not talk because he was called to an accident with injury. I said, "It's us." He was so quiet that I didn't know if he had heard me. In a choking voice, he said he'd be right there.

Stewart called the OHP headquarters and told them who the accident was and that he needed help. It wasn't long before there were patrol cars everywhere. Highway patrol is family, and family had been hurt.

The driver who hit us was drunk. He never saw us, and we hit him going sixty-five miles per hour. Stewart's parents both had concussions, broken bones, and a lot of cuts. They were hospitalized. The kids and I were treated and released.

I believe it was not time for any of us to be called home. If Craig had been sitting on Nanny's lap, he would have been crushed. Instead, just minutes before we were hit, Joyce handed him back to me. That simple act gave us twenty-six more years with Craig.

Holidays 2006

Since Craig died in January, our memories of Thanksgiving and Christmas are extra special. On Thanksgiving 2006, we had everyone at our house. It happened to be a beautiful day, and we were able to be outside after dinner.

For Christmas, we went to Clinton to see the grandparents. We took many pictures and are so thankful we did.

McKinney (2006)

After Christmas 2006, Craig and Des invited us to spend a few days with them. They also invited Christy's children (four, eight, and twelve at the time). They took Abby, Alex, and Zak to Six Flags over Texas. Since Izzie was only seven months old, we stayed home with her.

We had planned to leave on Thursday, but they asked us to stay another day. On Friday morning, Craig had an early flight. He came into our bedroom, hugged us, kissed us good-bye, and told us he loved us. That was the last time we ever saw him. His accident was the following Thursday. We are so thankful that God gave us that extra day, that extra hug, and that extra kiss.

We need to treat every day as if it is our last day. We have a guarantee of today but not tomorrow. Tell your family you love them and tell them often. Tomorrow might be too late.

They Grow Up Fast

No matter how old our children are, the time with them is precious. When our two children were small, a clerk said, "Enjoy them at this age. They grow up so fast." It stayed with me for all these years because it is so true.

Sometimes we get so wrapped up in our busy lives that we

get careless. When Craig was eight years old, the kids and I
went to church on a Wednesday night. Stewart met us there.
After church, Christy rode home with Stewart. Craig rode
with me. I stopped at the gas station, and Craig went in to
look at the video games. I went in to pay and drove home.
Stewart and Christy were just getting out of the car when
I pulled up. They both said, "Where is Craig?" I realized I
had left him at the gas station. We went back as quickly as
possible. I ran into the station, and he was watching someone
playing a video game. I thought he'd be devastated. I said,
"Craig, didn't you wonder where I was?" He said, "I thought
you were just getting a lot of gas."

About a year later, my aunt and uncle were celebrating
their fiftieth wedding anniversary at Clinton. Our family
met at my parent's house, and we walked to the church for
a special program in the sanctuary. I looked over at Stewart
and asked, "Where is Craig?" He was nowhere. I slipped out
and ran back to my folk's house. I ran in the house calling

his name. He answered from upstairs. He was watching TV and did not even know we had left.

From those experiences, I learned to slow down and enjoy the moment. We can get so caught up in our work, children's activities, and sports that we forget the moment. The following school year, we cut back where we could. The kids even took a year off from their activities. We had more fun that year. We would come home from school and have time to play. We made stone soup, we went out in the field, and drew pictures. We laughed and relaxed. The next year, we went back to our activities—but on a smaller scale. Life is so busy. Enjoy the moment.

When you are involved in outside activities, you might not realize how thin you have spread yourself until you leave a child at the gas station. If someone asks me to get involved in something, I say, "Let me think about it. I'll get back to you." That is a very honest answer. Giving myself time helps me make the right decision for myself and for my family.

We look back at the time we had with Christy and Craig

as children and have no regrets. God gives us our children on his time schedule. For some reason, it was in His plan that we only had Craig for twenty-six years. Treat your children today like there is no tomorrow.

Chaplain Sam Garner from the highway patrol said, "Lord, you have not promised us tomorrow, but you have given us today. Therefore, may we use the gift of this day wisely. Amen."

Tangible Memories

During the twenty-four hours we were looking for Craig's plane, we kept calling his phone. It went straight to voice mail. "Hey, this is Craig. Leave me a message, and I'll call you back." Family and friends left tons of messages. We began calling just so we could hear his voice. A friend of ours downloaded his voice so we can still hear it when we want to.

We still have many of his mementos in our house. We ran across a poem that Craig wrote in eighth grade for an English assignment. It was titled "The Day I Got Saved." We framed it.

He had been saved at an earlier age, and we have no doubt that he is in heaven. Reading his poem puts a warm smile in our hearts.

The Day I Got Saved

The day I got saved was a very special day.

The church and my family helped me along the way.

I'm glad I'm going to heaven and not to hell.

Because, after all, in heaven, we'll all be well.

If it wasn't for God, I wouldn't be here.

So that's why I thank him throughout the year.

I'm glad Jesus died for my sins,

So I can live a life of rejoice within.

Craig's Cross

Holidays were always very special for Craig, especially Christmas. When he was sixteen, he built a cross and put it on our hill. It's about six feet high, and he wrapped lights all around it. He would light it right after Thanksgiving, keeping it lit until New Year's Day. He would light it again the week before Easter.

After Craig's accident, we were gone three days. When we came home on Sunday morning, our neighbor had lit the cross as a reminder of Craig. To this day, the cross burns daily from dusk to dawn.

Craig Moments

Stewart and I run a hot shot service where we take refinery and oil field parts all over the country. These are some of our Craig experiences while traveling.

September 26, 2013

We were excited when we found we had a trip to Craig, Colorado. Even though it was September, they were already getting their fair share of snow. It was beautiful. After we delivered our load, we spent some time shopping in Craig. Of course, we had to get sweatshirts and mementos from Craig.

November 20, 2013

We pulled off the highway near Huntington, Indiana, to check our load. In the grass by a trailer wheel, we saw a little plane with a smiley face. The plane was clean and undamaged except for a little dew. We keep it on the dash of our truck. When we delivered the load to Cushing, Oklahoma, it was to a man named Craig.

July 18, 2014

Coming back from Utah, we were traveling along the mountains and a river. A small plane was traveling over the river right beside us. Then it sped up, turned around, and flew right over us. Craig used to do that when he was flying north from Texas. He would call ahead and say, "I'll be flying over your house around 1300 hours." We'd go stand in the front yard. He'd fly, circle a few times, wave his wings, and continue his journey. We picture his journey into heaven with him saying, "See you later, guys."

Craig's Inn

We were delivering a load to Louisiana on the main highway when we noticed it was unsteady. We took the next exit, checked the load and the trailer, and heard the most dreaded sound. The hiss of releasing air is never a good sound. Our tire was losing air. We pulled into the parking lot of Craig's Inn.

Not a day goes by that we don't think about Craig. We have reminders of him when we least expect them. I'm amazed by how often small planes fly overhead when we are out walking. We take that moment to say hi to him. We have both received comfort after "talking" to Craig.

Special Olympics

Stewart became involved with Special Olympics in 1984. When Craig was in third grade, he went with his dad to volunteer for Summer Games in Stillwater. They were hooked and volunteered throughout the years.

Stewart and I still have a passion for Special Olympics. We are always looking for ways to raise money and awareness for such an important cause. In 2001, I came up with the idea of walking 125 miles from Chickasha to Stillwater for Summer Games. Stewart said, "You've got to be kidding!" It is now an annual event with the highway patrol, family, and friends. Craig and Des walked with us many years. Christy and her family always meet us in El Reno.

The walk takes us six days. We average about twenty miles per day in three-mile legs. One of us walks while the other drives. Every three miles, we switch. What started out as Stewart and me with a highway patrol escort has turned into between ten and thirty people walking daily. Each day takes about ten hours. We either drive back to the house to spend the night or stay in a hotel.

We love every day of the walk. We take the side roads as much as possible, including Route 66. We have walked in the heat, near-freezing rain, strong winds, and perfect weather. The only thing we won't walk in is lightning or tornadoes.

Day One

We leave the Chickasha High School football field and walk to Minco. This year, when we arrived in town, a man met us with a fistful of Special Olympics medals. He told us they belonged to his special needs brother. His brother had passed away at the age of thirty. He didn't really know what to do with the medals and asked if we had a place for them. We proudly took them and told him the medals would become a part of our walk. We will carry his brother's medals on every walk.

Day Two

This is our longest day as we walk from Minco to El Reno to Yukon. One of our fondest memories is when a wheelchair athlete joined us. We told him we would parade through Yukon. He looked around and asked, "Where is the parade?" We told him, "You are the parade." The look on his face was priceless.

Day Three

We attend church at FBC Piedmont. Pastor Gary Caldwell used to be our pastor at FBC Ninnekah. It's worth the long walk to hear him preach. The church makes us feel like family and gives us the inspiration to keep going. After church, we eat lunch at the Sonic and take off from there.

We always think of Craig when we walk by the waste-treatment plant near Deer Creek. The first time he and Des walked with us, it happened to be their turn to walk by the plant. He kept the neck of his shirt pulled up over his nose to help with the stench. This happened for a couple of years—until he got smart and planned who would start walking that morning so it would *not* be their turn. We love having memories of Craig at different places. We never thought we would have a memory of him with a waste-treatment plant.

Day Four

Our walk leads into Guthrie. We always enjoy seeing the historic homes as we walk into town.

Day Five

This is one of our favorite days. Along Highway 77, we sometimes see a man spreading hay on his garden with a pitchfork. One year—on a Tuesday during school hours—we spotted three school-age boys fishing along the Cimarron River. Once the boys heard the OHP sirens and saw the lights flashing, they took off as fast as they could. Their fishing poles might still be at the river.

Day Six

This is absolutely our favorite day. We walk down Highway 51 and into Stillwater. So many buses with special athletes from all over the state pass us as they drive into Stillwater for Summer Games.

Day Seven and Eight

We stay in Stillwater and help with Summer Games. Every step we take to get there is worth it when we witness the determination of almost five thousand athletes.

May 2016 was our sixteenth walk to Stillwater. We've walked about two thousand miles. What a small struggle this is for us. We see a girl struggle with every step she takes, and she smiles all the way. We see a boy winning the wheelchair races for several years in a row. When he receives his gold medal, he gives it to the boy who came in second and says, "It was his turn to win."

In 1984, Stewart watched a young girl do a dance with a ribbon and a ball. He was amazed at how well she did, never missing the beat of the music or dropping the ribbon or the ball. Stewart asked her mother if he could meet the girl. She agreed but asked us to approach her carefully so we wouldn't scare her. The girl was blind and deaf.

Many of the athletes don't have a clue that they are

struggling because that is what their lives are like and that is who they are. We have learned so much from them. It gave us extra strength after losing Craig.

After Craig died, we began the "Craig Meyer Memorial Walk for Special Olympics." We wanted Craig's memory to live on. Many people wanted to join us on our walk to Stillwater but couldn't. It gave our community the chance to become involved.

In 2016, we held Craig's tenth annual walk at the high school football field. We have an average of eighty people each year. Everyone can walk one lap, one mile, or the entire three hours. Our whole family is involved and has a great evening. It's a win-win situation. We get to visit, exercise, and raise money for Special Olympics.

Photography credit Mike Cool

Front row: Abby, Christy, Beth Ann, Izzie holding Daddy Craig's picture,

Tinleigh, Deserae

Back row: Alex, Zak, Brandon, Stewart, Zack holding Owen

Craig Meyer Memorial Soccer Scholarship

Craig loved baseball, golf, and soccer. He played soccer through high school years and was the goalie on the Chickasha High School varsity team. Since soccer was such a big part of his life, we initiated the Craig Meyer Memorial Soccer Scholarship for a graduating senior. Craig's award helps toward college expenses and is presented every May. Izzie helps us present the award every year.

More Memories

In the Toilet

Craig was always a climber. When he was a toddler, he could easily climb out of his crib. One evening, I went to check on him—and he wasn't in his room. I heard splashing in the bathroom, and he was jumping up and down in the toilet. After I pulled him out, I got down eye level with him and gave him a lecture. He was really focused on me. I said, "Do you understand?" He reached up, grabbed my nose, and said, "Honk, honk."

My Shoes

I hate shoes and don't wear them unless I have to. While Craig and I were driving to Oklahoma City to meet Stewart at an award's luncheon, I carried my shoes to the car. When we arrived, I started to put on my shoes—but I only had one. The other was nowhere to be found because it had fallen in the driveway.

We drove to a shoe store, and I told Craig to run in and get a size 7 sandal. He got several, held them up at the window, and pointed at them to see which one I liked. He bought a pair for me, and we went on to the luncheon. He kept saying, "Do you like my mom's new shoes? Ask her why I bought them for her."

Flat Tires and Scary Movies Don't Mix (Stewart)

After we had gone to bed one night, the phone woke us up. Craig said, "Dad!" The only thing I could think of was that something had happened. I asked if everything was okay and where was he. He said, "I'm okay … sorta." I said, "What do you mean 'sorta'?" He was about two miles north of Des's house and had a flat tire. I asked why he didn't get out and change it. He said, "I don't think I can." I said, "What do you mean?"

He and Des had been watching scary movies at her house—and where he was stopped resembled a scene from the movie. He was scared and really wanted me to come out to help change his tire. I got up and drove out to where he was located. I pointed my lights to help him see the tire, and I watched him change it. When he asked why I wasn't helping him, I told him I was his protection. He shrugged and finished changing the tire. To the best of my recollection, the first time that story was shared was at his service.

Show and Tell

Stewart and I love motorcycles. After we got married, we each had one. Stewart had a 175 Harley, and I had a 125 Yamaha. I kept a box on the back of mine so I could take our five-pound poodle, Candy, on rides. We were married almost five years before Christy came along. After we started a family, having motorcycles didn't fit into the family plan. When Stewart retired, we decided it was time for our retirement vehicle. We bought a 2008 Ultra Classic Harley-Davidson motorcycle. When you purchase something new, it's always fun to show it to family. Our first trip was to Rush Springs to "show" Craig. It felt good to talk to him and let him know we were excited about something. Craig and our loved ones would be pleased to know that we are going on with our lives. Life is for the living. It's a difficult reality, but it's true.

Trial and Error

When Craig was about four years old, we went to the grocery store. Christy and Craig's favorite part of grocery shopping was purchasing popcorn from the machine when we finished. They put in a quarter, placed the cup under the dispenser, and the popcorn filled the cup.

I had always given Christy the quarter to get the popcorn, and she and Craig would share. This time, I gave the quarter to Craig. He put the quarter in the machine, placed the cup under the dispenser, and the popcorn knocked the cup on the floor—with all the popcorn. We went to the counter and got something to clean up the mess. Without a word, I gave Craig another quarter. He put it in the machine, placed the cup under the dispenser, and held it firmly. He proudly shared this popcorn with Christy.

When we lose a loved one, it is a learning experience as well as a tragedy, but we have to pick up our popcorn and keep going.

Two Steps Forward and One Step Back

When Craig was in elementary school, I took him and a friend to the mountains by Lawton. We drove to the base of Mount Scott. Our goal was to hike to the top. We made sure we had good climbing shoes, comfortable clothes, and water. We started climbing, but we could not just go straight to the top. We would get to one point and get stuck. We would have to move down and over and try another spot. At times, the three of us would go in different directions. Soon, someone would say, "Hey, let's try this way." We would all continue on together. There were a lot of two steps forward and one step back since we had to overcome boulders and other obstacles. Some parts were easier than others, but it was all difficult.

Four hours later, we reached the top. We celebrated.

However, the celebration was short because we knew we had to go back down.

Coming down was easier because we decided to take the winding road instead of climbing down. It took us about an hour and a half. Although it was still work, it was faster and smoother.

When we lost Craig, we didn't know how we would make it. We didn't know what to do. We didn't know how to go on. It was like climbing that mountain. We would think we were going in the right direction—until we would get hit with boulders and obstacles like his birthday, his angelversary, holidays, and Izzie's first dance recital.

For Craig's first birthday in heaven, the whole family got together and decided to celebrate his birthday at his favorite restaurant. "Hey, let's try this way."

We were prepared for our hike with shoes, comfortable clothes, and water. We had the essentials for a hike. The essentials for grief are faith, family, and friends.

Be prepared to take one step back. Just because we made

it to the top of the mountain didn't mean it was over. You never know what will set you back.

Try to stay focused on taking two steps forward. They may come in the form of a good memory, loved ones offering words of encouragement, or someone taking you to dinner. You can always reach out to God in prayer. If he can't get you those two steps forward, he will carry you.

CDL Test

Since Stewart and I started our hot shot service, we decided it would be beneficial for me to have my commercial driver's license. I passed my written test, but I was dreading taking my driving test. In fact, I waited eleven months—with one month to spare. My biggest fear was backing a thirty-six-foot trailer. Stewart was a great instructor, and on September 25, 2014, I decided not to put it off any longer.

We drove to Stillwater for the driving test. Stillwater will always be special because Craig and Des both graduated from

OSU. After Craig graduated, he became a flight instructor for the OSU flight school.

As we drove into the parking lot to test my backing skills, a plane similar to what Craig piloted flew over the parking lot. It didn't stop there. After my backing test, we drove around the streets of Stillwater, and the plane continued to fly over us. When we drove back to the parking lot, Stewart asked if I had seen the plane. Craig is always with us.

I passed my test and now have my CDL.

I had been dreading my driving test because of the trailer. Years ago, our lawn tractor was in the shop. They called at noon to let me know it was ready and would deliver it after work. However, I wanted to get the yard mowed that afternoon. I decided to pick up the mower myself. I hooked our eighteen-foot trailer to our 1980 Road Runner and drove the two miles into town. I parked and walked in to pay. While I was paying, the service man said he'd bring the mower around. He came back into the store and asked, "Where are you going to put the mower?" I said, "On the trailer." He said, "What trailer?" When I walked outside and looked, there was no trailer.

I didn't know what had happened to my trailer. I backtracked all the way home, but there was no trailer anywhere. All I could think about was how I was going to tell Stewart I had lost our trailer. He came home after work and said, "I was driving home and saw a red trailer out in the field that looks just like ours, but I knew it couldn't be." I had to confess. My mistake was not connecting the trailer once I put it on the ball.

Roller-Coaster Ride

We took a hot shot trip to St. Paul, Minnesota. After we delivered our load, we checked into a hotel. The desk clerk told us that we were within ten minutes from the Mall of America. I don't know which one of us was more excited to hear that information.

We went to the mall to have lunch and do a little shopping. Besides its size, the mall is famous for its indoor amusement park. There are three different roller coasters. After studying them, we picked the only one that didn't go upside down. We went through twists and turns, ups and downs, and even through a tunnel. That is exactly how we felt after Craig died. We went through shock, disbelief, crying, loss of energy, sadness, anger, frustration, and disappointment. Just like the roller coaster, a quick turn could change us from sadness to anger. The ups and downs could change us from tears to sullenness. Riding through the dark tunnel was something we went through for periods of time. We were so lost.

When we got on the roller coaster, an attendant went through each section to make sure we were seated and secure. At the end of the ride, the attendant was there to release us so we could be on our way. God also takes care of us from the beginning, through the rough times, and sees us on our feet to be on our way. And he *never* leaves us.

I Didn't Buy A Ticket For This Ride

Beth Ann Meyer

Why am I in this line?

My heart is hurting. My feet are heavy.

There is no exit. I can't go back.

I didn't buy a ticket for this ride.

The attendant clamped me in my seat.

Such a rough ride. All these ups and downs,

Sudden curves, and dark tunnels.

I didn't buy a ticket for this ride.

Will it ever end?

Can I get off now?

Do you hear me?

Finally, it is slowing down.

A hand reaches out to help me up.

As I depart the ride, I realize

I was never alone.

He had secured me in my seat.

It was his shoulder I leaned on.

He was the light in the darkness

He never left me.

Our Family Today

Christy and her husband Brandon, have three children. Zak and Alex are both in the army. Abby is in the eight grade. Des and her husband Zack, have Izzie, now in fourth grade. They also blessed us with Tinleigh, kindergarten and Owen, 2 1/2 years of age. We miss Craig so much, but we are so blessed to see our family continue to grow and remain close.

When we meet someone for the first time and visit for a while, they often ask, "Do you have children?" We used to dread that question. However, it has become easier. We say, "We have a daughter who is married with three children. We lost our son in 2007, but we still have our daughter-in-law and their daughter. Our daughter-in-law remarried, and they gave us another granddaughter and grandson." This way, Craig is still remembered—and it becomes a positive.

If someone asks about family in passing, we say, "We have two children and six grandchildren."

We have stayed very close to Des and her family. We celebrate birthdays and holidays. The grandchildren stay with us often. I realize not everyone is as blessed as we are. I was visiting with friends who lost their son. It's a battle for them to get to see their grandchildren. Our prayer is that anyone in that situation will see the blessings that can come from keeping that relationship strong.

We realize that our family is not typical. We proudly say that we have a daughter and son-in-law and a daughter-in-law and son-in-law.

Sitting: Beth Ann holding Owen, Grandma Edna,
Grandpa Leonard, Izzie, Tinleigh

Standing: Abby, Christy, Brandon, Zak, Alex, Belford, Stewart, Deserae, Zack

Daddy Craig

Since Zack adopted Izzie, she has a daddy in heaven and a daddy on earth. In order to avoid confusing her, we refer to Craig as Daddy Craig.

One day, Zack came over to pick up Izzie and Tinleigh. They were looking at Craig's picture and began arguing. Izzie said, "That's my Daddy Craig."

Tinleigh said, "No, that's *my* Daddy Craig." This went back and forth a few times. Finally, Zack laughed and said, "Girls, it's not a contest." There's no reason they can't both claim him.

Pool Party

Birthday celebrations are always fun. We celebrated Izzie's eighth birthday at the swimming pool. Izzie was swimming, laughing, and playing with her friends. I started thinking about how much Craig would have enjoyed watching his little girl grow up. I started to feel a little down until I looked over at Stewart. He and Zack were talking and laughing about something. It made me realize we were okay —and very blessed.

Christy

We met Zack not too long after he began dating Des. As hard as it was to not be able to see Des with Craig, we wanted her to be happy. And we knew she had found someone very special (even though he is an Oklahoma Sooner fan.) When we told Christy that she and Brandon needed to meet Zack, she said, "No."

About a month later, Abby spent the day with Izzie. Des and Zack brought Abby to Christy and Brandon's house. Des introduced Zack. Brandon was happy to have another OU fan coming into the family. Later, I said, "Christy, I thought you didn't want to meet Zack." She said, "This was fine. I just didn't want a planned meeting." I'm so glad we did not push her. It was God's timing—not ours.

Oklahoma University Fans Can Wear Orange

In August 2014, we planned a family trip to Arlington, Texas. Oklahoma State was playing Florida State at AT&T Stadium. Our family of twelve (including baby Owen), our friends Bob and Sheila of Fayetteville, Arkansas and one of their daughters Stacy spent the weekend together at the hotel and went to the football game on Saturday night. Des, Izzie, Stewart, and I are OSU fans. Zack, Christy, Brandon, Zak, Alex, and Abby are OU fans. Tinleigh and Owen either dress in orange or red, depending on which parent dresses them. That weekend, *everyone* wore orange and cheered for the Cowboys.

We are a nation divided in so many ways, including football teams, politics, and religion. Isn't it wonderful when we can come together? Aren't we lucky that God doesn't have a favorite color?

Alex, Zak, Brandon, Christy, Abby, Stewart, Beth Ann
holding Owen, Deserae, Izzie, Zack holding Tinleigh
Not pictured: Bob, Sheila and Stacy Suvino

Deserae's Letter

I remember January 4, 2007, like it was yesterday. It was the day my world was turned upside down and my heart was ripped into pieces. Never would I have ever dreamed that I would lose my husband at only twenty-four years old. Craig and I were high school sweethearts. We met on a church trip to Six Flags in the summer of 1997, fell in love, and from that moment on, were inseparable. Craig was one of a kind. He was one of the nicest and most well-respected people I'd ever met. He had such a positive outlook on life and never had a bad word to say about anyone. Everyone who met Craig immediately liked him. It didn't take me long to realize that this was the guy I wanted to marry! I knew he'd be a great husband and father, and I loved his family. After we graduated from high school, we attended OSU together. During our time at OSU, we were married in Eureka Springs, Arkansas, in June of 2003. After we graduated, we moved from Stillwater, Oklahoma, to McKinney, Texas, where we began our careers and soon found out that we were pregnant! Our daughter Isabella (Izzie) was born in June 2006. What a blessing she was to both of us! We were so in love and wanted to spend every moment we had with her. Craig loved to stay up and read her bedtime stories, which was what he was doing the night before he left for his final flight. He read her a story about a little girl losing her teddy bear. I wonder now if that was a sign of what was to come.

I remember coming home from work, picking up Izzie, and being excited that Craig was coming home since he had been gone for a few days. Living in Texas, I didn't have any family close by and hadn't made many friends yet since we had only lived there a short time. I was always anxiously awaiting his return. I remember getting out of the car to go inside, looking up at the sky, noticing how cloudy it was, and wondering if they had made it back okay. Craig should've been home by dinnertime, and when he wasn't, I started to get worried. I received a call from his company a short time later, letting me know that they were concerned about him and the other pilot since they hadn't made it back or heard from them. I immediately panicked and called my family and Craig's family to let them know. They began the trek from Oklahoma to Texas to be with me. I also called the flight company and asked them for the other pilot's wife's phone number so I could talk to her. What a blessing it was to be able to talk to someone who was going through exactly what I was going through at the time. As the night went on and Craig and the other pilot hadn't checked in, search crews were sent out to begin looking for them. We stayed up all night long, praying and anxiously waiting for good news that they had found them alive. Unfortunately, good news was not to come.

As Beth Ann and I were making our way to Arkansas the next day to join the search crews, we received a call from Stewart, letting us know that they had found the plane and there were no survivors. I asked Beth Ann to pull the car over. I can't describe the feeling I felt at that moment other than complete numbness and total shock. It was like my mind couldn't process that much pain at once. Kind of like when they say you lose a limb your body goes numb and you don't feel it at first? That was what it was like. I didn't believe it; my soul wouldn't let me believe it because the pain was too great for it to bear at that moment. A little part of me died that day along with him. That's what happens when you lose a spouse; your souls are united in marriage, and then when they die, a part of you leaves with them.

I truly believe that, when loved ones pass, they leave us signs here on earth to let us know that they are okay and are always with us. My sign from Craig was crosses. Craig always loved crosses. He made a cross when he was younger to put up on the hill behind his parents' house. He loved to draw crosses all the time and even carried one in his wallet that said "Jesus" on it. The accident happened on a hill overlooking a valley. After we arrived at the crash site and looked over the wreckage, we took a break and walked out to the edge of the hill only to see a cross lit up on top of a church on the other side of the valley, shining brightly through the fog. At that moment, I knew that Craig had arrived at his heavenly home. Although the pain from losing him was excruciating, seeing that brought me comfort.

After leaving the crash site, my family returned to McKinney to help me pack my things to move back to Oklahoma. On the trip back, crosses kept jumping out at me from everywhere. Before the accident, I would occasionally notice crosses here and there, but on the way home, it was like they were making themselves obvious to me. I knew, without a doubt, that God and Craig were at work, letting me know they were there for me.

After the funeral, the shock wore off and the pain from losing Craig really set in. When you lose a spouse, you experience a loneliness like no other. The person who you used to sleep next to every night and share every detail of your life with suddenly isn't there anymore. For the first couple of months, I merely just existed. I wasn't living at all. I was just going through the days like a zombie. I remember attending a wedding shortly after the accident, and I just couldn't bring myself to be happy for the couple. I was so angry at God for letting my husband die. Why did anyone else deserve happiness when I was living a nightmare? It didn't take long for me to realize that I couldn't keep going like that. I needed to be there for my daughter since I was the only remaining parent she had on earth. She deserved more than the parent I was being at the time. Reality was just too painful to bear. I remember praying to God and asking him to carry me. I could no longer walk on my own two feet and needed him to carry me through life for a while. You know what? He did!

Slowly, God began putting the pieces of my life back

together. Step one was finding a job so I could support Izzie and me. Although I had a great job in Texas that I loved, I knew I needed to leave it and move back to Oklahoma to be with my family. God found me the perfect job where I could do what I loved to do, make new friends, and pour my energy into projects to get my mind off of things. Somewhere in the midst of working and raising a child, I guess God decided that I shouldn't be alone. Zack entered my life. After Craig passed away, I doubted I'd ever get married again, but God had other plans for me. The day I knew Zack was the one was the day we took Izzie on her first date with us. Zack was so good with her and loved her like his own daughter. Izzie immediately took to Zack and had a blast with him that night. I knew from that moment on that it was meant to be. When you lose a spouse, you definitely need to wait a while before entering another relationship—but don't be afraid to ever date again or remarry. I can't imagine not having Zack in my life. He is a wonderful husband and father to our three children. It feels great to be able to be happy again and spend the rest of my life with a wonderful man.

I'll never forget the night I first took Zack to meet Stewart and Beth Ann. He was quite nervous on the way over there about what they would think of him, but I assured him that they were the most easygoing and loving people in the world—and everything would be fine. The night went great with all of us laughing together and having a good time. On the way home, he said I was right that they really were incredible people and that he felt a love and compassion in them that transcended heaven and earth. I told him that night that they would always be a part of Izzie and my life— no matter what. Zack said he wouldn't have it any other way. Whether it was Zack seeking Stewart and Beth Ann's approval for the adoption of Izzie or the heartfelt conversation we had with them about always being in our children's lives— when Zack and I found out we were pregnant, we wanted to make sure they knew just how important they were to us. We are so blessed to still be close to Stewart and Beth Ann, and we always will be. When your spouse passes away, it is so important to remain close with their parents and keep the relationship strong.

It is now coming up on the tenth anniversary of the tragedy that forever changed all of us. I've never felt God's presence as strongly as I did in the first year after the accident. He revealed himself to me in so many ways, and although I don't miss the grieving process, I sometimes miss feeling him carry me (although I know he is always there to do it again if I ever need him to).

For those who are grieving, the best advice I can give is to let God carry you through your time of need. Although January 4, 2007, will always be a painful memory for me, it taught me so much. I've learned that it doesn't do any good trying to find answers about why bad things happen. Instead, try focusing your energy on trying to find God. I'll never understand why Craig had to leave this life so early. I'm sure we will all get answers in heaven one day, but for now, we all really miss him and look forward to reuniting with him.

Luckily for us, he continues to reveal himself through Izzie daily—and we are so thankful for that. Craig was such an incredible person, and I know God is using him in big ways in heaven. That brings me comfort until we see him again one day.

For those dealing with grief, fully surrender your life to God and let him carry you. I have found that it is the only way to get through a terrible tragedy. We, as human beings, just aren't equipped to get through something like that on our own. Let God carry you until you are able to walk again. Then, let him lead you.

Deserae, Izzie, and Craig
Photography credit Kathy Wenzel

Craig and Izzie

Tinleigh, Deserae, Owen, Zack, and Izzie

Photography credit Cami Benecke

Christy's Letter

My brother. My life mate. My "practice" child. My secret keeper. My friend. My tattletale. My last nerve. My favorite hug. My protector. My hero.

I was hysterical … bawling. My daddy called to give me the worst news I had ever gotten. I felt it the night before but couldn't give in to reality. I felt Craig. I knew he was with me. I still prayed that God would help us find him … alive. I begged. I know I was being selfish, but he was my brother— my only sibling. He still had so much to do in life. He was supposed to be here for the rest of *my* life. He supported me in every decision I made, and I supported him just as much. I screamed at my dad, "No! No! Not Craig! Not Craig … it's not fair! No! Why?"

My dad, with a quivering voice said, "I know. I know." His voice left. I could hear him crying. He couldn't talk anymore. His friend picked up the phone. As much as I appreciate the love and support he gave my family, I heard five words I have promised myself I would never say to anyone: "Be strong for your family." That was it for me. I locked up like Fort Knox. I shut down and buried my feelings. I became a robot. I went through denial and anger, but I didn't grieve. I needed to make sure everyone else was okay. I needed to be there for them. That's what I was told to do. I had never been in that position. I had never been the rock. I didn't have a choice.

Huge mistake. After a few months, I was wearing down. I was trying to jump my own hurdles with my own little family while still putting on my strong face. Behind that strong face was a broken heart.

Please listen. This is my only advice after losing a very close loved one. Be there for yourself first. If you can't go through the normal grieving process, you can't be strong for those around you. You have to go through all stages: denial, anger, bargaining, depression, and acceptance. I'm not saying you can't be there for each other, but please don't try to be the rock. There's no such thing. Our families are in this together ... to support and love each other, and most of all, to hug and pray for each other. Don't try to fake strong.

Weakness is okay in times like this. God is your strength.

Lean on him. God will only give you what you can handle?

No. I don't believe that. In those times, let him carry you.

Photography credit Glamour Shots

Kathy Wenzel's Letter (Craig's Mother-in-Law)

The first thing that comes to mind as I think about losing

Craig is God's peace. Every mother wants to fix things and

protect their children from harm and fear. There was absolutely

nothing any of us could do to help Craig or Deserae. We had

to give it to God. We all talked about where they might be and what they might be doing, hoping for the best. We all prayed for God to bring comfort and peace to everyone.

I prayed for the safety of everyone as I held that precious baby, wondering what the news would be before I answered each phone call and each knock at the door. When the sad news came, I fell to my knees, hugging Izzie. Hearing that Craig had died, I prayed and asked God to help us all. He did. Immediately I felt a warm sense of peace, and I knew God was wrapping his arms around us.

If you have never experienced God's warm hug of peace and comfort, it is the most amazing feeling you will ever have. It is still difficult, but he gives us strength and comfort to go on—and he continues to bless us in so many ways. Craig was an extraordinary special young man. He was especially kind, giving, and God loving! God continues to bless us in so many ways. Izzie reminds us of Craig with her big heart and compassion and wanting to always help others.

Compassion is a gift from God, and Craig left a legacy of love and compassion … thanks to God's peace and comfort!

Jon Hansen (Stewart)

I had asked my best friend, Jon Hansen, to write a chapter for our book. At the time, Jon had just begun his battle with cancer. On April 15, 2016, Jon went to be with our Lord and Savior.

I had the distinct privilege of speaking at his celebration of life. And it was a true celebration of life. He touched so many lives, not just in Oklahoma—but all over the nation and world. What an inspiration he was to so many.

I mentioned several experiences I called *Jonisms*. A Jonism would be defined as a way of positively affecting someone else's life.

When we received notification that Craig's plane was missing on January 4, 2007, Jon dropped everything and flew to Batesville with me, reassuring me that we would find Craig, even if it took calling out FEMA Task Force I.

The next morning, he went with an Arkansas State Police helicopter pilot and said they would be up as soon as the weather cleared. They were. They found the plane approximately one mile from the south end of the runway. There were no survivors. When Jon made it back to the airport, he handed me his pocketknife and said, "Keep this. I used it to cut Craig's seat belt."

He built a bed of leaves on the ground, gently removed Craig from the plane, and laid him on the bed.

Later that day, we went to the crash site. Jon showed us (family and friends), where he had laid Craig and introduced us to the investigator. The investigator was very thorough and answered everyone's questions.

Jon rented a van for of us to travel to Des's home in McKinney. On the way there, we organized Craig's celebration of life on McDonald's napkins. At Craig's celebration of life, there was a large yellow wreath. At first glance, it appeared to be yellow roses. It was made of mustard packets. Guess who it was from?

There are several Jonisms in this chapter. This is how a friend pays it forward. He continued to check on my family and me until the day he went to heaven. My family and I were so blessed to have Jon as my best friend. Thank you for your love and compassion for so many.

What can you do in a time of loss? Pick a Jonism and pay it forward.

Tom Boyt's Letter

Where to begin? As a boy, we didn't know Craig nearly as well as we knew Christy—for several reasons. First and foremost, Craig was a boy! We have three daughters.

Our story with Craig really began when he took the job with the oil pipeline company. He was assigned the duty of flying the pipeline in a small aircraft for security purposes. One day, while sitting in my office at Valparaiso University, my assistant told me I had a call from Craig Meyer and asked if I wanted to take it. It took a few seconds for it to sink in who was on the other end of the phone, and then it hit me.

Craig Meyer! "Of course I will take this call." It was a very unusual phone call for me. Most young people would never call some old guy they haven't seen in many years out of the blue. I had never received such a phone call before, and I have not received one since. But Craig was different. So to hear from Craig Meyer was a real treat and a very pleasant surprise. We chatted on the phone for quite a while, and we had a nice conversation. He told me that he and the other pilot would be spending the night in Valparaiso, Indiana. I asked him if he would like to have dinner with Janice and me. He readily accepted. I asked him how he knew we lived in Valparaiso, and he said he thought he had remembered that we had moved there. He had called his dad to find out for sure and to ask him if he thought it would be okay to call. He was staying at the Courtyard by Marriott in Valparaiso, which was the nicest hotel in town. His plane was parked at the Porter County Airport, which was within view of his hotel.

Craig's flight that day into Valpo would become a routine flight for him every two or three weeks. He and another pilot would fly from Arkansas, check the pipeline, land and refuel in Valparaiso, and stay overnight. The next day, they would fly up into Michigan and then back across Indiana into Illinois and then back to Arkansas. It was great to know this meeting with Craig would not be a onetime event. I would pick him up from the Courtyard that evening, and the three of us would go to a restaurant that was right across from his hotel. We decided on Kelsey's, which is a steakhouse. I had given Craig his choice of where to go, and he was sure Kelsey's would be great. He wanted prime rib! At about six o'clock that evening, Janice and I picked up Craig at the hotel.

The thing I remember most was his big smile. He always was a very friendly kid, and nothing had changed. He was just as friendly and outgoing as ever. Maybe more. We drove to Kelsey's, looked at the menu, and I suggested the prime rib. He jumped at it and ordered a huge slice of prime rib. We spent the time chatting and catching up. We found out that Craig was married to Deserae and spent time looking at "thousands" of pictures of her on his phone. He was clearly very much in love, very proud of her, and was missing her while his job forced him to be away from home. This became routine for his visits. We would go to Kelsey's for prime rib, and he would bring new pictures to show us of Deserae and later baby Izzie.

He was always very emotional when he talked about Deserae and Izzie, and most times, he would shed tears. He would just beam when he talked about anyone in his family. It was obvious that Desi was the love of his life—at least until Izzie came along! He also spent a lot of time talking about his dad and how he wanted to be just like him. It was also clear that he had a very strong relationship with Jesus, and we had long talks about that as well. He was truly a faithful man, and it was clear right from the beginning that he didn't just talk about his faith—he lived it. It was an amazing time to witness. We had dinners like this every two or three weeks. It was wonderful.

Let me now move to the night prior to his fatal flight. It was a normal night like the many times when he was in town.

He called me at work, and we set up a time for me to pick him up. Of course, he wanted to go to Kelsey's for prime rib. That particular night, he seemed melancholy. Something was just not right with him. I started asking him questions and tried to get him to open up a bit and tell me what was going on. As usual, he showed us pictures of Deserae and Izzie. While he bubbled as he showed us the pictures, he also cried. He just couldn't stand being away from them. He said that he really needed to find work where he could be at home with his two girls every night. That really started the conversation and got things rolling. He opened up and started talking about his life. He talked about where he was, what he wanted in life, and where he was headed. I asked him what kind of job he wanted the most, and he talked about flying corporate jets. He said that those jobs were pretty hard to find, and even if he did find one, they did not pay very well. We all laughed about the money when he told us what he was making in his current job. He said that the only reason he was working in his present job was to build up enough flight hours to apply for a position as a corporate pilot.

Craig and I talked for quite a while about being a corporate pilot, and I asked him if anything else would be of interest that would be better for his family. He talked for a brief time about maybe taking a job where he didn't fly. This surprised me because I know how much he loved to fly and how proud he was of his Oklahoma State experience. He didn't dwell on that option very long. It was clear that not flying was not really an option.

I asked about flying for the Oklahoma Highway Patrol and following in his dad's footsteps as a state trooper.

He was very proud of his dad. He had actually considered that and thought it would be really cool because they had some great aircraft that he could fly and that he could combine flying and serving in a way that he could not while running security checks on an oil pipeline.

I asked about taking a good look at the OHP and talking with his dad after he got home from this trip.

From what he knew, it would take too long to move into the role as an OHP pilot. He thought he would have to train to become a state trooper first and then work toward a pilot position. It would take a few years in the OHP before he could fly.

I told him that the longer he waited to start, the longer it would take to get into the cool aircraft. Even while training and being a state trooper, he could continue to get flight hours. "If you start now, in a very short number of years, you'll be flying for the Oklahoma Highway Patrol. My philosophy has always been to just get started. The sooner you start, the sooner you finish."

He agreed but mentioned that Desi had discouraged working for the OHP because it was too dangerous.

I leaned over the table, looked Craig in the eyes, and said "Craig, how could working for the Oklahoma Highway Patrol be any more dangerous than what you're doing right now?"

He chuckled.

I said, "Your dad was a state trooper for what, thirty years or more, and during that time, how many times did he have to draw his gun?"

Craig responded that, to his knowledge, he had drawn his gun either never or maybe once—and that he had never had to fire it in the line of duty.

I asked Craig how safe it was for him to be flying in a small, single-engine aircraft at five hundred to a thousand feet off the deck through all kinds of weather and over all kinds of terrain. "What happens if you lose power or hit a severe downdraft or severe turbulence?"

He got very serious and started reciting the restart checklist.

I said, "Craig don't forget who you are talking to. I know the checklist. If you're five hundred feet off the deck, how much time do you think you have to restart your engine?"

He continued being very technical and talking about doing this or doing that.

I said, "It all depends on where you are when a critical event takes place because, no matter what, you know you're going down. Everything depends on whether you are over a canyon or over houses or over a forest. You are going in, and there's really not a lot you can do about it."

He looked at me in a strange way that I hadn't seen before, shook his head, and said, "Yeah. That's true."

We talked about his job and the company.

He said the other pilot was a good guy. They talked about their families all the time, and the only thing either of them wanted was to get home to be with their families.

I asked him about the rules for flying in bad weather and aircraft maintenance issues.

He said that the company, of course, set the guidelines for flight and the safety rules.

I asked if the company had ever told him to fly when he didn't think it was safe.

He said absolutely not. The policy was that the final decision on whether to fly or not due to weather conditions or maintenance issues was totally the pilots' decision.

I asked him if that had happened in the past where they had dangerous flight conditions and had decided not to fly.

He said that it had happened—and they grounded themselves due to weather conditions and had to stay an additional night. He said the company did not question the decision.

Janice said she needed to get home and left. Craig and I left for the hotel. We talked in my truck under the canopy of the hotel for couple more hours.

At the end of the evening, Craig looked at me and said, "Tom, I think this is the last trip I will be making up here for the company."

I told him that I truly hated to hear that because we loved having him there—but I understood. I asked him to stay in touch with us and told him that we would love to meet his wife and baby girl. I mentioned that the weather forecast for the next day was not good and to let me know if he was still in town.

He assured me that he would.

I told him that I had to be in West Lafayette for a meeting the next day. "If you do leave tomorrow, when you get down toward West Lafayette, waggle your wings for me. I'll be watching. I know you won't see me, but if the timing is right, I might actually get to see you. Just know that I'll be waving back at you."

He laughed and said he would.

With that, we hugged and he got out of the car.

The morning of January 4, 2007, it was thirty-seven degrees, very windy, and cloudy—and it looked like rain. I expected to hear from Craig after I got back in town that night. I figured we could continue our conversation and share another prime rib. As I drove south to my meeting, the weather got worse. It was very windy, and it was pouring. I kept my eyes up in case I saw a small single-engine aircraft flying low under the clouds, but I did not see him.

I went to my meeting and then drove home. I got home about five o'clock, anticipating a phone call from Craig. I did not receive a phone call, but I really wasn't worried. I assumed that they had gone ahead and taken off. They both desperately wanted to get back home to see their families.

Something inside me told me to check my e-mail. I saw the e-mail from Beth Ann with the subject line: "Pray for Craig." I will never forget that e-mail. I don't remember where I was when Kennedy was assassinated. I don't remember where I was when the World Trade Center buildings came down. I will never forget where I was when I read that e-mail.

After recovering from the shock of the e-mail, I went into our barn and got some equipment together for hiking or riding or whatever was necessary to help in the search. I threw it in my truck and headed for Arkansas. I got as far as Bloomington-Normal before I got a phone call from my daughter. Shoni had heard from Christy that they had found the crashed plane. Craig and the other pilot had not survived. I turned around and came home.

Craig and I had many conversations about a lot of things. He was a very spiritual man, and he lived his faith. He loved his God, his family, and his work. It was a blessing to have him in my life. I knew him as a boy, and I knew him as a man. I know he touched a lot of lives in his short time here on earth. I consider myself one of the fortunate ones he touched.

Heaven is a better place with Craig in it, but I still miss him.

The purpose of these letters was to give some insight into Craig's life and to let people understand what an effect one person can have on so many different people.

The CRAIG Plan

The death of a loved one is never easy. We developed the "CRAIG Plan" to help get through the tough times.

- Commit
- Reflect
- Accept
- Include
- Grieve

Commit to one day at a time—or even an hour at a time.

Every day, we ask God to get us through the day. Every night, we thank him because he did. Nighttime seemed to be the worst because we couldn't shut down our minds and go to sleep. Mornings were the worst because it would seem like a normal day—and then it immediately hit us that Craig was gone. Don't ask more of yourself than you are able. Give yourself a small window for the future.

Reflect about your loved one.

It was so hard to talk about Craig without crying. The more we talked about him, the easier it got to say his name. We had so much company in the first few days. Being with family and friends was wonderful, but a few days before the service, we needed time to get our thoughts together about our memories of Craig. We went to Des's family's cobblestone house out in the country. We spent the afternoon sharing stories of Craig and writing them down. We cried, but we also laughed. We shared the stories at his service. Talking about your loved one will get easier as time goes on.

Accept the help, love, and prayers from family, friends, and even strangers.

We received a card from a family in Batesville. They had heard about our son on the news. So many people are on the giving end, and it's hard to be on the receiving end—especially in tragic situations. We learned to accept those gifts. Every offer was like a small dose of medicine. It helped the hurt a little at a time.

Trust in God and lean on him. We cannot do this on our own, and he does not want us to.

Include your loved ones.

It may be as simple as saying, "Craig would have loved this." If someone asks about your family, it's okay to say you've lost a loved one.

Grieve

Grieving is part of the healing process. That sounds so cliché, but it is true. If you need to cry, yell, or hit a punching bag, do it. It's like children holding their breath when they are mad. Eventually, they have to let go. Many times, the ones who need to grieve the most don't think they can. They feel they need to be the strong ones in the family. There is no strong one in the family at times like that. You can be there for them—but also let them be there for you.

Craig's Story

We hope this book will help those who are grieving. We want
to help others learn how to deal with friends and family who
are grieving.

About the Authors

Stewart and Beth Ann Meyer have been married since November 26, 1971. Stewart grew up in Oklahoma City and moved to Clinton, Oklahoma, in 1958.

Beth Ann grew up on a farm in Corn, Oklahoma, and moved to Clinton in 1966.

Even though they lived in the same town, they didn't meet until 1970. Stewart drove a red 1967 Barracuda, and Beth Ann drove a gray 1962 Volkswagen bug. Like all teenagers during that time, they would drag main, honking and waving at those passing by. Beth Ann was drawn to the red Barracuda.

One day, Stewart called Beth Ann and said, "This is Stewart Meyer. I'm the one who drives the red Barracuda. Would you go get a coke with me?"

Beth Ann said, "Yes." She thought she would finally get to ride in that car. They were married a year and a half later.

After they were married, Stewart worked as a police officer, and Beth Ann taught school. Christy was born in Clinton in 1976. In 1978, Stewart joined the Oklahoma Highway Patrol. This led to their move to Chickasha. Craig was born there in 1980.

Stewart retired from Oklahoma Highway Patrol after twenty-nine years. Beth Ann retired from teaching after thirty-two years. After a few years of retirement, they went for a new career together. They own and run a hot shot service, taking parts for refineries and oil fields all over the country. It gives them a chance to travel and see the country.

The Meyers are involved in their church at First Baptist in Chickasha. They also enjoy volunteering for Special Olympics. Stewart is the president of the Retired Oklahoma Troopers Association.

They enjoy spending time with their six grandchildren. Their daughter Christy and family live in El Reno. Their daughter-in-law Des and her family live in Chickasha.

Photography credit Abby Schroeder

Printed in the United States
By Bookmasters